The Workplace You Need: Spiritual Warfare Prayers That Silence Evil Powers At Your Workplace.

Johannes Tefo

Published by Johannes Tefo, 2024.

Also by Johannes Tefo

Family spiritual Warfare Books
Youth's Guide To Spiritual Warfare
A Women's Guide To Spiritual Warfare

Standalone
Deliver Your Soul From Evil
Overcoming Spirit Of Stagnation
The 24: Prophetic Word For This Season 2024 And Beyond
Michael For Warfare
Territorial Spirits: Overcome Evil Strongholds in Your Life And
Take Over Your Community With Strategic Warfare And Winning Prayers
Prayers Against Suicide Spirit
Spiritual Warfare When Enough is Enough
Identity In Christ
Prayers Against Satanic Networks
The Workplace You Need: Spiritual Warfare Prayers That Silence Evil Powers At Your Workplace.

Table of Contents

I dedicate this book to the body of Christ and people in general who are going through challenges in their lives, especially at the workplace. God is bigger!

Introduction

After a careful study and reading from the prophetic book of Daniel, I have found out that what set Daniel and his friends from the rest was his devotion to his God that he went as far as ditching the Babylonian way of culture, food, way of Babylonian life and system. As a prophetic individual myself, I can without a doubt tell you that some food we consume has a spiritual effect on our bodies. For instance, you will not last for an hour in prayer when you had junk food like pizzas and hamburgers.

As much as we consume spiritual food, which is the word of God—spiritual diet is as important as well. There is a whole new revolution right now about which diet to go for, what to include and not. The Bible will always be our number one go-to regarding life choices. Daniel ate fruits and vegetables and drank water too. It is as simple as ABC. I have never seen a pale, drained, or exhausted individual with a diet plan like this. The man, Daniel was ten times better than the men of all Babylon in wisdom, knowledge, and understanding.

The Babylonians saw Daniel as the god. No one could articulate and divide the mysteries behind the Word of God like Daniel. Bear in mind that, Babylon was the land of astrologists, Diviners, sorcerers, witches, and wizards.

Jeremiah 50:1-2

The word that the LORD spake against Babylon and against the land of the Chaldeans by Jeremiah the prophet. 2 Declare ye among the nations, and publish, and set up a standard; publish, and conceal not: say, Babylon is taken, Bel is confounded, Merodach is broken in pieces; her idols are confounded, her images are broken in pieces.

Isaiah 47: 1-8

1 Come down, and sit in the dust, O virgin daughter of Babylon, sit on the ground: there is no throne, O daughter of the Chaldeans: for thou shalt no more be called tender and delicate. 2 Take the millstones, and grind meal: uncover thy locks, make bare the leg, uncover the thigh, pass over the rivers. 3 Thy nakedness shall be uncovered, yea, thy shame shall be seen: I will take vengeance, and I will not meet thee as a man. 4 As for our redeemer, the LORD of hosts is his name, the Holy One of Israel.

5 Sit thou silent, and get thee into darkness, O daughter of the Chaldeans: for thou shalt no more be called, The lady of kingdoms. 6 I was wroth with my people, I have polluted mine inheritance, and given them into thine hand: thou didst shew them no mercy; upon the ancient hast thou very heavily laid thy yoke. 7 And thou saidst, I shall be a lady for ever: so that thou didst not lay these things to thy heart, neither didst remember the latter end of it.

8 Therefore hear now this, thou that art given to pleasures, that dwellest carelessly, that sayest in thine heart, I am, and none else beside me; I shall not sit as a widow, neither shall I know the loss of children: 9 But these two things shall come to thee in a moment in one day, the loss of children, and widowhood: they shall come upon thee in their perfection for the multitude of thy sorceries, and for the great abundance of thine enchantments.

These two scriptures give a clear picture of the Babylon culture and how evil and corrupt the nation was. Imagine how much more Daniel and his friends faced in their daily provincial duties at the workplace. These men of God almost lost their lives due to evil conspiracy, deceit, and manipulation. But when the oil of God is upon you—you will mount up with wings and fly—you will always come out the other side.

You can be tried even through the fire, but when you walk with Christ, the fire losses its power in your flesh. In fact, the fire makes you purify you and promotes you to your greatness. Take a dive into these three men, Shadrack, Meshach, and Abednego. Even a hint of smell over their clothes was not found. No smoke aroma was in them because they were covered by the hand of GOD!

GOD IS NOT GOD ON SUNDAY but God of every day. The principle here is to publish the name of your God wherever you are. Even at work, they must be aware that your aura is the representation of the heavenly kingdom. Many fall short because when they are at work, they hide Christ.

Daniel denied Babylonian food because they would have defiled his belief. Life is spiritual. We put spirituality above all things—the rest shall follow. Serious spiritual warfare takes place at the workplace because if the enemy can make you unhappy and drain your strength, even at home you will still come that energy which will also affect your marriage. 70% many people spent it at work. Therefore, your work environment should be welcoming to you, Child of God.

I started this chapter with the importance of a spiritual diet. It goes to say "Your health is your wealth". And your spiritual diet is everything. Because strength comes from the secret place conversing with your Creator. A prayer lifestyle is paramount. However, I also touch upon the food that we eat, literally. Some people call it the "Daniel diet" or "Daniel fast". Either way, we can see that the result of great men and women starts off with what men or women eat. Because the whole matrix of food is connected to your mental health, mental performance, and spiritual strength.

This is not a theory, eating healthy is healthy living. Healthy bodies are bound to be productive at work. And your eyes of understanding open, and becomes clearer when you are in a healthy space in all aspect of your life. Spiritual warfare is a whole different thing, as it encompasses various weapons to dismantle the powers of evil. The Lord at some point in life revealed to me the importance of healthy food in connection with Daniel's lifestyle.

The sacrifice he made while in the kingdom of Babylon stood the time. In a foreign land, whereby its laws and traditions are unfavorable to your situation, it is a great deal to stand on the ground of your own belief. Throughout history, Jews have been persecuted and hated for their belief in God. You can study the patterns from Egypt to Babylon to the present day, the hate still persists. It just shows you that when you are all about God, you become the enemy of everyone. The first principle of making in the workplace is your prayer lifestyle. The power of prayer cannot be diminished anywhere. No one can block a serious prayer from a faithful child of God. Even the prince of Persia would not!

The unseen realm is real

A man is a spirit first. God the Creator saw us in His vision plan before we were even created. If He knew Jeremiah before He was born, surely He saw you before you were conceived. We serve the powerful God who is not constrained by time and space. In the eternal realm of God, there is no time. For a day is like a thousand years before the Almighty God.

Everything gift we have, you and I, was placed in us before the foundation of the world. That even the Devil Himself was doing God's work by nailing Christ on the Cross. The spirit of Satan was operating in the Leaders of that time. You and I are not supposed to fear the enemy but to recognize that he is behind the majority of destruction in our lives. Many of us are still waiting for Christ to take the Devils out of our marriage, workplace, community, churches, etc. while authority and power are being placed over the body of Christ.

We as believers possess the high power that even the saints of old wished as if they were living in our times. This is the end times folks whereby the Devil is working timelessly because his time is running out. The angels of the Living God also ascend and descend from heaven with the gospel of Christ—ministering unto those who shall inherit the salvation of God.

Therefore, at the workplace, the negative energy will drain you if have not developed a serious prayer lifestyle. I am talking about demons which are unclean spirits of greed, lust, and many more. The sad truth is that, if the founder of the business is not in Christ, then he is in someone else other than Christ. One famous preacher once said, if the leader is not a follower of Christ, then he is a follower of the world. The follower of the world is the enemy of God. It is not typical for employees to start off with prayer in the morning before duty calls.

As a young man coming straight from university, I used to yearn and pray—asking God to bless me with different kinds of jobs in the corporate world. It is common to dream of working in a certain company. One day I had a vision of the company I wanted to work for, and I saw that the owners of that particular company had made a covenant with the Devil, that they have sacrificed souls in the earliest stage. Usually, people do this evil tiding for money, power, and influence. This is common in all parts of the world. Just imagine for a second working in that kind of environment.

I am just trying to tell you that prayer is the most important investment you can make in your life. The eyes of your understanding open up—and you start to discern what is good and acceptable. Because in this day and age, good and evil are mixed all together. This is the nation that Isaiah will condemn in the age to come, white is back, black is white. The theme of this chapter is an emphasis that life is spiritual. By looking at things from a spiritual point of view, we will gain so much knowledge, wisdom, and understanding.

When you are fighting with your co-worker at a workplace, look at it from a different angle, and from where the conflict emanates from. Mapping things from a spiritual point of view will save many from beating the air. However, I am not saying that all fight occurs in the spirit realm, but the majority of them do. Jealousy spirit is the toll of many conflicts in the workplace. Not also neglecting Jezebel and her hordes of other demons; control, power, greed, lust, pornography, immorality, etc.

The unseen realm affects us more than what we see. Things don't just happen; they take shape in the spirit realm before they manifest in the physical. Prophecy is a medium used to transfer the goodness of the Lord to his children. You receive the Word before manifestation. Faith is the engine that keeps you going, trusting the Lord even in difficult situations where you see no way out.

Witchcraft at the workplace is real

There is so much happening in workplaces, the spirit of darkness is taking its toll. When other co-workers see you being favored, it becomes a thorn in their flesh. Many have lost their lives due to things like this. Prophet Daniel was one of those individuals who went through hard times because certain jealous individuals were against him. I always tell many that, when the oil of God is upon you, it does not only attract beautiful things but also the bad.

The Devil is after the chosen. You and I are chosen by God to advance his will on earth. We will be persecuted, hated, and even some will be excommunicated. My grandfather was cursed with swelling feet that caused his knees to be cut by a woman who saw that his boss loved him more than her. From jealousy and unnecessary competition at the workplace come things like this. Many go to sorcerers and diviners to excommunicate others from their jobs through demonic spells and charms. This is a global thing right now—it is no longer an African thing.

My tribe in South Africa is widely known for being powerful and dangerous when it comes to the dark science—witchcraft. And it is not mainly because of poverty or anything, people just go into it willingly just to hurt their rivals. 90 percent of families are broken—no longer on good terms because of some jealous aunt or uncle who just decided to cast the spells for fellow family members because they are advancing in life while he is not. We can see that jealousy is the root of much evil.

How can you explain it when a graduate from university spends more than 10 years to 15 years jobless? It is purely evil. Many are the victim of circumstance. It is through the power of prayer and working with the holy spirit that reveal all things that we may conquer. We are more than conquer but at the same time, it is up to us to deal with the evil. God cannot come down from His throne to cast out demons. Authority is laid upon the church to advance the kingdom of God.

———

YOU HAVE AUTHORITY and power to tread upon wickedness. For you are backed by the real power from heaven. The heavenly angels of God walk with you, even though you may not see them with physical eyes, they are there to protect you and lead you to your promised land.

You can tap into their power through prayer. Your body will always send signals if angels are around.

Psalm 34: 7

7 The angel of the LORD encampeth round about them that fear him, and delivereth them.

Hebrews 1:14

14 Are they not all ministering spirits, sent forth to minister for them who shall be heirs of salvation?

1 kings 19:7

7 And the angel of the LORD came again the second time, and touched him, and said, Arise and eat; because the journey is too great for thee.

Factors of spiritual warfare

The only power that the enemy has against the body of Christ is **Words!**

• The battlefield is your **Mind**. It is the door whereby the enemy enters into your territory.

• The Kingdom of God is voice activated for there is power in our **Tongue** when we boldly proclaim God's promises in His Word, as we bind and loose spirits in Jesus Name! (Prov. 18:21)

• It is the **Spirit of God** that leads us and empowers us whenever are in battle against the enemy. For us to be led and empowered by God, we need to be continually plugged into the Source of our power.

Increased prayer lifestyle

Increased prayer lifestyle, means you grow every day in prayer, you pray better than you prayed last night each day. Even if you do not feel like it, just pray. The body may not be willing but the spirit is willing. Prayer is the ultimate weapon that delivers us from things seen and unseen. If God can open our eyes to show us what the impact of our prayers does, we will be out of breath!

Prayer travel in space and time, by the speed of light to clear your way and your path. The Lord God blesses us and fills our cups in sight of our enemies, therefore, a prayer lifestyle is ideal to survive the ordeal of the enemy. You may fight that He wants to promote you at your work, but you have to know that promotion comes through the fire. You have to go through the fire like Shadrack, Meshack, and Abednego for your promotion. Standing in God and resting in His promise is enough for you.

We live in a society where it is normal to adopt cultural trends and it is the societal norm. but you as the child of the Most High—our cultural and traditional values lie upon the rock of ages—Christ. The Living Word of God should direct our everyday situation, at work, in our community, and family. The Word of the Most High is enough, has always been enough since the beginning of times, and does not change. You can never dilute the Word of God. Rest in the Word and in the promises of God.

We all know that is not easy to pray. However, the altar that we stand on is solid, we stand on the holy altar that was laid by the saints of God—Christ Himself being the head of the household of believer's.

The increased prayer lifestyle will open your eyes to your understanding. The world calls it the third eye—we call it the eyes of the spirit, the spirit of knowledge, understanding, and wisdom. This is the highest level of an individual—living the life directed by the Holy Spirit of God and ministering angels. Whereby you see things from the heavenly perspective than from a natural realm.

You will excel in everything you do just like Daniel who had an excellent spirit upon him. At your workplace, the spirit of excellency and favor is what you need. This does not come from your boss but from God.

Daniel 1:17-20

17 As for these four children, God gave them knowledge and skill in all learning and wisdom: and Daniel had understanding in all visions and dreams. 18 Now at the end of the days that the king had said he should bring them in, then the prince of the eunuchs brought them in before Nebuchadnezzar. 19 And the king communed with them; and among them all was found none like Daniel, Hananiah, Mishael, and Azariah: therefore stood they before the king. 20 And in all matters of wisdom and understanding, that the king enquired of them, he found them ten times better than all the magicians and astrologers that were in all his realm.

Daniel and his three friends were ten times better than the wise men of Babylon because they spent time in the secret place with their God—not just any other God but the God of the universe. Babylon is a land of idol worship—but these men stood on the ground of their faith even in workplaces where many will be lenient at work in their faith. We see believers hiding their faith when at work.

Serious battles are won at our knees. Three times a day, Daniel will pray! Many of us are in the position of Daniel, I bet we will slack off just because of the responsibility that comes through the work. You will find many spending their time in corporate neglecting the majority of things even their spiritual need merely because "they are busy".

Daniel 6:3

3 Then this Daniel was preferred above the presidents and princes, because an excellent spirit was in him; and the king thought to set him over the whole realm.

The favor was upon Daniel because an excellent spirit was on him. Daniel was backed by the army of heaven. Earthy wisdom is nothing compared to walking in the holy spirit of God. The man who knows His Creator is bound to change the world around him. Well, this is what Daniel did. He introduced the Living God in a pagan society, the then known world knew about the powerful God of Israel through Daniel. This man spends four decades in four kingdoms. An excellent spirit is derived from spending time in the secret place with God. Three times a day He will pray. We can learn from this great saint of God.

Before work Guideline

Pray first in the morning

Morning prayers start your day afresh. This is the best attitude we can make to start with an offering of thanksgiving and praise to the Most High for protecting us. We remind God how fortunate and blessed we are to be His children born of spirit and water. Throughout my experience, I have learned that praying first in the morning will guide how your day goes. God deserves the first, therefore, before we go about our daily activities, we have to acknowledge His presence in our lives.

Here are various scriptures that talk about praying early in the morning. Our Lord Jesus Christ used to pray in these early hours. Early morning prayers are the powerful starters of your day. God deserves our first in all things. It is being obedience and thankful for adhering to early morning devotional.

Psalm 5:3 - "My voice shalt thou hear in the morning, O LORD; in the morning will I direct my prayer unto thee, and will look up."

Psalm 88:13 - "But unto thee have I cried, O LORD; and in the morning shall my prayer prevent thee."

Psalm 143:8 - "Cause me to hear thy lovingkindness in the morning; for in thee do I trust: cause me to know the way wherein I should walk; for I lift up my soul unto thee."

Isaiah 50:4 - "The Lord GOD hath given me the tongue of the learned, that I should know how to speak a word in season to him that is weary: he wakeneth morning by morning, he wakeneth mine ear to hear as the learned."

Mark 1:35 - "And in the morning, rising up a great while before day, he went out, and departed into a solitary place, and there prayed."

Luke 21:38 - "And all the people came early in the morning to him in the temple, for to hear him."

John 8:2 - "And early in the morning he came again into the temple, and all the people came unto him; and he sat down, and taught them."

Acts 5:21 - "And when they heard that, they entered into the temple early in the morning, and taught. But the high priest came, and they that were with him, and called the council together, and all the senate of the children of Israel and sent to the prison to have them brought."

1 Thessalonians 5:17 - "Pray without ceasing.

Develop an attitude toward Thanksgiving

Dear believer, starting your day with an attitude of thanksgiving and prayer can have a transformative impact on your life. It sets the tone for the day ahead, aligns your heart with God's will, and allows you to experience His presence and guidance throughout the day. Here are some simple yet powerful tips to encourage you in this journey:

1. **Create a Sacred Space:** Designate a special place in your home where you can have some quiet time with God. This could be a corner in your room or a cozy spot in the garden. Make it comfortable and free from distractions so that you can focus solely on connecting with your Creator.

2. **Set a Consistent Time:** Try to wake up a little earlier to allow yourself enough time for prayer and thanksgiving. Setting a consistent time each morning helps establish a routine, making it easier to cultivate a habit of starting your day with God.

3. **Begin with Gratitude:** As you wake up, take a moment to express thankfulness for the gift of life, for the new day ahead, and for all the blessings in your life. Cultivate a heart of gratitude by remembering the goodness of God in both big and small things.

4. **Use Scriptures as Your Guide:** The Bible is a rich source of inspiration and guidance. Select a few verses

that resonate with you and use them as prompts for your prayers and meditations. Reflect on their meaning and apply them to your life.

5. **Pray for Others:** Intercede for your loved ones, friends, and even those you might consider your enemies. Praying for others fosters compassion and helps you see beyond your own needs, bringing you closer to God's heart of love for all people.

6. **Keep a Prayer Journal:** Consider maintaining a journal to jot down your prayers, thoughts, and reflections during your morning time with God. It allows you to track your spiritual growth, remember God's faithfulness, and revisit the answered prayers.

7. **Use Prayer as a Time of Surrender:** Lay your burdens and worries before God. Surrender your plans and desires to His will. Embrace the peace that comes from knowing you are not alone in facing life's challenges.

8. **Practice Mindfulness:** Be present in the moment during your prayer and thanksgiving time. Avoid rushing through it. Instead, cultivate a mindful awareness of God's presence and listen to what He might be speaking to your heart.

9. **Pray with Expectation:** Approach your morning prayer and thanksgiving with a sense of expectation. Trust that God hears you and will respond in His perfect timing and wisdom.

10. **Sing and Praise:** Incorporate worship songs or hymns into your morning routine. Singing praises to God uplifts your spirit and prepares your heart to receive His word.

11. **Seek God's Word:** After your prayer time, spend a few moments reading and meditating on scripture. Allow God's Word to speak to you and shape your thoughts and actions for the day.

12. **Be Patient with Yourself:** Developing a habit of morning thanksgiving and prayer takes time. Don't be too hard on yourself if you miss a day or struggle to maintain consistency. Be persistent and remember that God's grace is always available to you.

In conclusion, dear believer, starting your day with an attitude of thanksgiving and prayer is a beautiful way to draw closer to God and experience His love and guidance. With these practical tips, you can cultivate a morning routine that enriches your spiritual life and sets the foundation for a day filled with peace and purpose. May your mornings be filled with joy as you deepen your relationship with the One who loves you beyond measure.

EARLY MORNING WORD Study

Studying the Word of God early in the morning before going to work can be a rewarding and enriching experience. Here are some practical tips to help you make the most of your study time:

Set a Regular Time: Choose a consistent time each morning to study the Bible. Waking up a little earlier can provide you with a peaceful and uninterrupted environment for your study.

Create a Comfortable Space: Designate a quiet and comfortable space where you can focus on your study. Whether it's a corner in your room or a cozy spot in the living room, make sure it's free from distractions.

Start with Prayer: Begin your study time with prayer, asking God to open your heart and mind to understand His Word and apply it to your life.

Have a Plan: Decide on a specific reading plan or a book of the Bible to study. This will give your study purpose and direction, ensuring you cover meaningful passages.

Use Study Guides or Devotionals: Consider using study guides, devotionals, or commentaries to help you gain deeper insights into the Scriptures and understand their historical and cultural contexts.

Take Notes: Keep a journal or notebook to jot down your reflections, insights, and questions during your study. This practice helps you remember and apply what you learn.

Engage with the Text: Read the Bible with an active mindset. Ask yourself questions about the meaning of the verses, the context, and how they relate to your life.

Meditate on Verses: Select a verse or a passage that resonates with you, and spend some time meditating on its meaning and how it applies to your life.

Apply the Word: Consider practical ways to apply the lessons you learn from the Bible in your daily life, especially in your work environment.

Use Audio Versions: If you have limited time in the morning, you can listen to audio versions of the Bible while getting ready for work or during your commute.

Involve Others: Consider studying the Bible with a friend or joining a small group Bible study. Sharing insights and discussing the Word with others can deepen your understanding.

Stay Consistent: Developing a habit of studying the Word takes time and discipline. Stay committed, even on days when you feel less motivated.

Be Patient and Open: Be patient with yourself as you grow in your understanding of the Bible. Stay open to new revelations and allow the Holy Spirit to guide you.

Prioritize Application: Don't study just for knowledge; aim to apply the principles and teachings of the Bible in your life. Let the Word transform your attitudes and actions.

End with Gratitude: Before you head to work, take a moment to thank God for the insights gained during your study and ask for His guidance throughout the day.

Remember, studying the Word of God is a journey of deepening your relationship with Him. As you commit to studying early in the morning, you'll find that it positively influences your perspective, decisions, and interactions in your workplace and beyond.

Scripture about work productivity

Proverbs 14:23 - "In all labour there is profit: but the talk of the lips tendeth only to penury."

Colossians 3:23 - "And whatsoever ye do, do it heartily, as to the Lord, and not unto men."

Ephesians 4:28 - "Let him that stole steal no more: but rather let him labour, working with his hands the thing which is good, that he may have to give to him that needeth."

Proverbs 12:11 - "He that tilleth his land shall be satisfied with bread: but he that followeth vain persons is void of understanding."

Proverbs 21:5 - "The thoughts of the diligent tend only to plenteousness; but of every one that is hasty only to want."

2 Thessalonians 3:10 - "For even when we were with you, this we commanded you, that if any would not work, neither should he eat."

Proverbs 13:4 - "The soul of the sluggard desireth, and hath nothing: but the soul of the diligent shall be made fat."

Proverbs 10:4 - "He becometh poor that dealeth with a slack hand: but the hand of the diligent maketh rich."

1 Corinthians 15:58 - "Therefore, my beloved brethren, be ye stedfast, unmoveable, always abounding in the work of the Lord, forasmuch as ye know that your labour is not in vain in the Lord."

Proverbs 22:29 - "Seest thou a man diligent in his business? he shall stand before kings; he shall not stand before mean men."

These verses emphasize the importance of diligence, hard work, and dedication in our endeavors, reminding us that productivity is not only beneficial for our own well-being but also a way to honor God with the talents and opportunities He has given us.

Spiritual warfare Prayers

Jabez prayer of breakthrough

1. Heavenly Father, I come before You with a humble heart, seeking Your favor and blessing just as Jabez did. (1 Chronicles 4:10)
2. Lord, enlarge my territory and expand my influence for Your kingdom's sake. (1 Chronicles 4:10)
3. Father, bless me indeed, according to Your abundant grace and mercy. (1 Chronicles 4:10)
4. Grant me wisdom and understanding, that I may walk in Your ways and make wise decisions. (Proverbs 4:7)
5. Lord, keep me from evil and protect me from harm and temptation. (1 Chronicles 4:10)
6. Help me to be a person of integrity, following Your commandments and living a righteous life. (Psalm 119:1)
7. Father, let Your hand be upon me, guiding and leading me in all that I do. (1 Chronicles 4:10)
8. Lord, grant me success in my endeavors, that I may bring glory to Your name. (Joshua 1:8)
9. Give me a heart filled with compassion and love for others, that I may be a blessing to those around me. (1 Corinthians 13:4)
10. Help me to forgive those who have wronged me and extend grace and mercy, just as You have forgiven me. (Matthew 6:14-15)

11. Lord, grant me the courage to step out of my comfort zone and trust You to do the impossible in my life. (Philippians 4:13)

12. Father, teach me to pray without ceasing and seek Your presence daily. (1 Thessalonians 5:17)

13. Help me to seek first Your kingdom and righteousness in all my decisions and priorities. (Matthew 6:33)

14. Lord, fill me with Your Holy Spirit, empowering me to walk in the fruit of the Spirit. (Galatians 5:22-23)

15. Father, guide me in using my gifts and talents to serve others and bring glory to Your name. (1 Peter 4:10)

16. Grant me divine opportunities to share the gospel and be a witness of Your love and grace. (Acts 1:8)

17. Lord, help me to be persistent in prayer and not lose heart. (Luke 18:1)

18. Give me the grace to persevere through trials and challenges, knowing that You are with me. (James 1:2-4)

19. Father, grant me a heart of thanksgiving and praise, even in difficult circumstances. (1 Thessalonians 5:18)

20. Help me to trust in Your timing and not lean on my understanding. (Proverbs 3:5-6)

21. Lord, grant me divine favor and open doors of opportunity that no one can shut. (Revelation 3:8)

22. Father, let my life be a living testimony of Your goodness and faithfulness. (Psalm 107:1)

23. Help me to be diligent in my work and faithful in my responsibilities. (Proverbs 22:29)

24. Lord, protect me from the snares of the enemy and lead me away from temptation. (Matthew 6:13)

25. Grant me a heart of humility, putting others before myself and serving with love. (Philippians 2:3-4)

26. Father, help me to walk in purity and holiness, fleeing from sinful desires. (1 Thessalonians 4:7)

27. Lord, give me discernment and wisdom to make godly decisions in my relationships. (Proverbs 13:20)

28. Help me to be content with what I have and trust in Your provision. (Hebrews 13:5)

29. Father, let me be a vessel of peace and reconciliation, seeking unity among believers. (Ephesians 4:3)

30. Lord, grant me a heart of compassion for the lost and a burden for their salvation. (Romans 10:1)

31. Help me to be a person of prayer, seeking Your face and interceding for others. (Ephesians 6:18)

32. Father, fill me with Your joy, which is my strength, and let it overflow to others. (Nehemiah 8:10)

33. Lord, let my life reflect Your love and mercy, drawing others to You. (John 13:35)

34. Grant me the courage to take risks for Your kingdom and step out in faith. (Hebrews 11:6)

35. Help me to be patient and wait on Your timing, trusting that Your plans are perfect. (Psalm 27:14)

36. Father, grant me a heart of obedience, willing to follow Your will and direction. (1 Samuel 15:22)

37. Lord, help me to be diligent in studying Your Word, that I may be equipped for every good work. (2 Timothy 3:16-17)

38. Grant me a heart of generosity, willing to give freely and sacrificially. (2 Corinthians 9:7)

39. Help me to be quick to forgive and show grace to those

who have hurt me. (Ephesians 4:32)

40. Father, let Your peace that surpasses all understanding guard my heart and mind. (Philippians 4:7)

41. Lord, grant me humility to seek wise counsel and receive correction when needed. (Proverbs 12:1)

42. Help me to be a person of integrity, standing firm in the truth and resisting deception. (Proverbs 10:9)

43. Father, let my words be seasoned with grace, bringing encouragement and hope to others. (Colossians 4:6)

44. Lord, grant me a heart that seeks after You and desires to know You more. (Psalm 42:1)

45. Help me to walk in the fear of the Lord, acknowledging Your sovereignty and authority. (Proverbs 9:10)

46. Father, grant me a heart of humility and meekness, following the example of Christ. (Philippians 2:5-8)

47. Lord, fill me with a spirit of unity and cooperation, seeking to build up the body of Christ. (Ephesians 4:3)

48. Help me to be a person of faith, trusting in Your promises and believing in Your goodness. (Hebrews 11:1)

49. Father, grant me the grace to forgive myself for past mistakes and embrace Your forgiveness. (1 John 1:9)

50. Lord, let my life be a living sacrifice, holy and pleasing to You, for Your glory. (Romans 12:1)

May these prayers inspired by the story of Jabez ignite a passion for seeking God's favor and blessing in your life, as you walk in faith, obedience, and love.

PRAYER FOR EXCELLENCY at your work

1. Heavenly Father, I come before You today, seeking Your guidance and wisdom as I strive for excellence in my work. (Proverbs 16:3)
2. Lord, grant me a diligent spirit to perform my tasks with enthusiasm and dedication. (Proverbs 22:29)
3. Help me to work as unto You, knowing that I am ultimately serving You and not just my earthly employer. (Colossians 3:23-24)
4. Lord, let my work be a reflection of Your character, displaying honesty, integrity, and sincerity. (Proverbs 10:9)
5. Fill me with creativity and innovative ideas to solve challenges and improve processes in my workplace. (James 1:5)
6. Grant me the ability to work harmoniously with my colleagues, showing love and understanding. (Romans 12:16)
7. Father, help me to maintain a positive attitude, even in the face of difficulties, knowing that You are with me. (Psalm 46:1)
8. Lord, give me the strength and endurance to overcome obstacles and complete my tasks with excellence. (Philippians 4:13)
9. Help me to be a reliable and trustworthy employee, fulfilling my responsibilities with excellence. (Luke 16:10)
10. Heavenly Father, bless the work of my hands, and may it prosper under Your favor. (Psalm 90:17)

11. Lord, grant me wisdom to make sound decisions that lead to success in my endeavors. (James 1:5)

12. Help me to be disciplined and avoid distractions that hinder my productivity. (Proverbs 21:5)

13. Lord, let me be a source of encouragement and inspiration to my colleagues. (1 Thessalonians 5:11)

14. Father, grant me humility to accept constructive feedback and use it to grow and improve. (Proverbs 12:1)

15. Help me to be proactive in seeking opportunities for professional development and learning. (Proverbs 18:15)

16. Lord, protect me from the temptation of laziness and procrastination. (Proverbs 6:6-8)

17. Grant me favor in the eyes of my supervisors and coworkers, that I may be a positive influence. (Proverbs 3:4)

18. Help me to manage my time wisely, prioritizing tasks according to their importance. (Ephesians 5:15-16)

19. Lord, fill me with confidence and assurance in my abilities, knowing that You have equipped me for success. (Philippians 4:13)

20. Father, grant me the ability to communicate effectively and build strong relationships with clients and customers. (Proverbs 16:23-24)

21. Help me to maintain a spirit of excellence, always seeking to improve and go the extra mile. (Daniel 6:3)

22. Lord, give me the grace to handle stress and pressure with grace and composure. (Psalm 55:22)

23. Grant me the humility to acknowledge my mistakes

and take responsibility for them. (Proverbs 28:13)

24. Lord, bless my workplace with harmony, unity, and a spirit of cooperation. (Psalm 133:1)

25. Help me to set achievable goals and pursue them with determination and perseverance. (Philippians 3:14)

26. Lord, let me be known for my integrity and strong work ethic. (Proverbs 20:7)

27. Father, guide me to use my skills and talents for the betterment of my workplace and society. (1 Peter 4:10)

28. Grant me the ability to adapt to changing circumstances and stay flexible in my approach. (Ecclesiastes 3:1)

29. Lord, let my work bring honor and glory to Your name, shining as a light in the darkness. (Matthew 5:16)

30. Help me to be proactive in seeking solutions and not dwelling on problems. (Philippians 4:8)

31. Lord, grant me wisdom to identify and seize opportunities for growth and advancement. (Ecclesiastes 9:10)

32. Father, I pray for favor in the eyes of clients and customers, that they may trust and value my work. (Proverbs 3:3-4)

33. Help me to be a peacemaker in my workplace, resolving conflicts with love and patience. (Matthew 5:9)

34. Lord, grant me the ability to meet deadlines and fulfill my commitments. (Psalm 37:5)

35. Heavenly Father, bless my workplace with prosperity and success, that we may be a blessing to others. (Deuteronomy 28:12)

36. Help me to be proactive in seeking feedback and

learning from those with more experience. (Proverbs 19:20)

37. Lord, protect me from the influence of negative attitudes and gossip in my workplace. (Ephesians 4:29)

38. Grant me the courage to step out of my comfort zone and embrace new challenges. (Joshua 1:9)

39. Help me to maintain a balanced life, prioritizing family, health, and spiritual well-being. (Mark 8:36)

40. Lord, fill me with joy and contentment in my work, knowing that I am fulfilling Your purpose for my life. (Ecclesiastes 5:19)

41. Heavenly Father, I pray for divine connections and opportunities that align with Your will for my career. (Psalm 75:6-7)

42. Help me to be patient in times of waiting and trusting in Your perfect timing. (Psalm 27:14)

43. Lord, grant me the ability to think critically and solve problems effectively. (Proverbs 2:6)

44. Guide me in using my resources wisely and being a good steward of what You have entrusted to me. (1 Peter 4:10)

45. Help me to be a servant leader, seeking to empower and support those I work with. (Matthew 20:26-28)

46. Lord, grant me the courage to take calculated risks and step into new opportunities. (Isaiah 41:10)

47. Father, I pray for divine inspiration and creativity in my work projects. (Exodus 31:3)

48. Help me to maintain a spirit of thankfulness, recognizing that every good thing comes from You. (1 Thessalonians 5:18)

49. Lord, grant me the ability to persevere through challenges and setbacks. (Romans 12:12)
50. Heavenly Father, I commit my work to You, seeking Your guidance and blessing each step of the way. (Psalm 37:5)

May these prayers inspire you to seek excellence and productivity in your workplace, knowing that your efforts are not in vain when done for the glory of God.

Prayer for influence

1. Heavenly Father, I come before You with a humble heart, seeking Your guidance and favor in my workplace. (Proverbs 3:5-6)
2. Lord, grant me wisdom and understanding, that I may lead with discernment and insight. (Proverbs 24:3-4)
3. Help me to be a person of integrity and character, reflecting Your light in my actions and decisions. (Matthew 5:16)
4. Father, fill me with the fruit of the Spirit, that others may see Your love, joy, and peace in me. (Galatians 5:22-23)
5. Lord, grant me the ability to build strong and meaningful relationships with my colleagues and superiors. (Proverbs 18:24)
6. Help me to be a servant leader, following the example of Jesus, who came not to be served but to serve. (Mark 10:45)
7. Father, grant me the grace to be a positive influence, encouraging and empowering others to reach their

potential. (1 Thessalonians 5:11)

8. Lord, give me the courage to stand firm in my faith and convictions, even in challenging situations. (1 Corinthians 16:13)

9. Help me to communicate effectively and with grace, using my words to inspire and uplift those around me. (Colossians 4:6)

10. Father, grant me divine opportunities to share Your gospel and be a witness of Your love and grace. (Acts 1:8)

11. Lord, let my actions and attitudes be a reflection of Your love, drawing others closer to You. (John 13:35)

12. Help me to be a peacemaker, resolving conflicts with humility and understanding. (Matthew 5:9)

13. Father, grant me the wisdom to lead with humility and seek counsel from You and others. (Proverbs 11:2)

14. Lord, let my work ethic and dedication inspire others to give their best in their tasks. (Colossians 3:23-24)

15. Help me to be a source of encouragement, lifting up those who are discouraged or weary. (1 Thessalonians 5:14)

16. Father, grant me the ability to remain calm and composed in stressful situations, trusting in Your sovereignty. (Psalm 46:10)

17. Lord, give me discernment to identify and seize opportunities for growth and positive change. (Ephesians 5:15-16)

18. Help me to be generous and willing to share with others, using my resources to bless those in need. (1 Timothy 6:18)

19. Father, grant me the courage to speak up for what is right and just, even when it is unpopular. (Proverbs 31:9)

20. Lord, let my humility and willingness to learn make me approachable and relatable to my colleagues. (James 4:10)

21. Help me to be a problem solver, offering creative and effective solutions to challenges at work. (Philippians 4:13)

22. Father, grant me the grace to forgive those who have wronged me and show them Your love. (Matthew 6:14-15)

23. Lord, let my character and integrity be a shining example to others, drawing them to seek Your ways. (Titus 2:7-8)

24. Help me to be patient and understanding, recognizing that each person has their own struggles. (Colossians 3:12)

25. Father, grant me the ability to handle conflicts and differences with grace and humility. (Ephesians 4:2-3)

26. Lord, let my words be seasoned with grace, bringing encouragement and hope to those around me. (Ephesians 4:29)

27. Help me to be a good listener, showing empathy and compassion to those who share their burdens with me. (James 1:19)

28. Father, grant me divine insights and understanding that I may offer valuable contributions to my workplace. (Daniel 5:14)

29. Lord, let my dedication to excellence inspire others to

strive for greatness in their work. (Colossians 3:23)

30. Help me to be patient and kind, treating everyone with respect and dignity. (1 Corinthians 13:4)

31. Father, grant me the courage to take initiative and lead in areas where I can make a positive impact. (Joshua 1:9)

32. Lord, give me the ability to adapt to change and challenges, trusting in Your faithfulness. (Hebrews 13:8)

33. Help me to be a team player, cooperating and supporting my colleagues to achieve common goals. (Ephesians 4:16)

34. Father, grant me divine favor in the eyes of my superiors and colleagues. (Proverbs 3:4)

35. Lord, let my actions speak louder than my words, showing the love of Christ to all I encounter. (1 John 3:18)

36. Help me to lead by example, demonstrating humility and vulnerability in my leadership. (Matthew 20:26-28)

37. Father, grant me the wisdom to prioritize tasks and manage my time effectively. (Psalm 90:12)

38. Lord, let my life be characterized by gratitude and thankfulness, giving glory to You in all things. (1 Thessalonians 5:18)

39. Help me to be a person of vision, leading with purpose and direction. (Proverbs 29:18)

40. Father, grant me the grace to be a mentor and support to others, helping them grow in their careers. (Titus 2:3-5)

41. Lord, give me the strength and endurance to persevere through challenges and obstacles. (Isaiah 40:31)

42. Help me to be fair and just in my decisions, treating all with impartiality. (Proverbs 20:7)

43. Father, grant me divine insight and discernment to identify and seize opportunities for growth. (1 Chronicles 12:32)

44. Lord, let me be known for my kindness and compassion, reflecting Your love to those around me. (Ephesians 4:32)

45. Help me to be a person of prayer, seeking Your guidance and wisdom in all aspects of my work. (Philippians 4:6)

46. Father, grant me the grace to admit my mistakes and take responsibility for my actions. (Proverbs 28:13)

47. Lord, let me be a light in my workplace, pointing others to You through my words and deeds. (Matthew 5:14)

48. Help me to be a peacemaker, promoting unity and harmony among my colleagues. (Romans 12:18)

49. Father, grant me the courage to step out in faith and share my faith with boldness. (Acts 4:29)

50. Lord, let my life be a living sacrifice, holy and pleasing to You, for Your glory. (Romans 12:1)

May these scriptural prayer points empower you to seek God's favor and influence in your workplace, as you lead with humility, wisdom, and love.

Prayer for protection

Heavenly Father, I come before You in the name of Your Son, Jesus Christ, seeking Your protection at my workplace from evil people who may seek to harm or deceive me. I acknowledge that You are my refuge and strength, and I trust in Your unfailing love and care.

Lord, I pray that You would surround me with Your divine hedge of protection, as mentioned in Job 1:10. Guard my heart and mind with Your peace, so that I may not be shaken by the schemes of the wicked.

In the authority of Jesus Christ, I rebuke every spirit of darkness and evil that may try to infiltrate my workplace. I declare that no weapon formed against me shall prosper, as Your Word assures us in Isaiah 54:17.

Father, I ask for discernment to recognize those who may have malicious intentions, and grant me wisdom to navigate challenging situations with Your grace and truth. Help me to stand firm in the face of adversity, knowing that You are with me and will never leave nor forsake me.

Lord, shield me from the deceitful tongues and harmful actions of evildoers, and let their plans be brought to nothing. Let Your light expose the darkness, as stated in Ephesians 5:13, so that evil works may not prosper around me.

I pray for a hedge of protection around my colleagues and supervisors, as well. May Your angels encamp around us, guarding us from harm and guiding us in Your ways.

Lord, fill me with Your Holy Spirit, so that I may respond to negativity and hostility with love and forgiveness, as Your Word instructs in Matthew 5:44. Help me to overcome evil with good, trusting in Your justice and recompense.

I choose to put on the whole armor of God, as described in Ephesians 6:10-18, to stand strong against the wiles of the devil and evil people. Grant me the strength to resist temptation and to cling to righteousness.

Thank You, Father, for being my protector and shield. I trust in Your promises and rely on Your unfailing love. In Jesus' name, I pray. Amen.

Prayer for spiritual strength

1. Heavenly Father, I come before You, seeking spiritual strength and guidance in my workplace.
2. Lord, fill me with Your Holy Spirit, empowering me to face challenges with confidence and grace.
3. Grant me the wisdom to navigate work-related decisions with discernment and understanding.
4. Help me to stay focused on You, Lord, and not be overwhelmed by the demands of my job.
5. Father, strengthen my faith and trust in Your divine plan for my life and career.
6. Lord, guard my heart and mind against negativity and temptations that may arise at work.
7. Enable me to be a shining light of Your love and truth in my workplace.
8. Lord, grant me the courage to stand firm in my

convictions and uphold Your principles.

9. Help me to find moments of stillness and reflection amidst the busyness of work.

10. Father, equip me with spiritual discernment to recognize and resist any ungodly influences.

11. Lord, surround me with like-minded believers at work, that we may encourage and support one another.

12. Grant me the strength to forgive and show grace to those who may mistreat or offend me.

13. Help me to be diligent in prayer, seeking Your guidance and strength throughout the day.

14. Father, shield me from the pressures of the workplace, and let Your peace reign in my heart.

15. Lord, keep me grounded in Your Word, that I may find strength and comfort in its truths.

16. Help me to prioritize my spiritual well-being, knowing that it impacts every aspect of my life.

17. Lord, enable me to be a source of encouragement to my colleagues, lifting them up in prayer.

18. Father, let my actions and speech reflect Your love and kindness to all I encounter.

19. Strengthen my resolve to live out my faith boldly, even in the face of opposition.

20. Lord, grant me the ability to forgive myself for mistakes and grow from them.

21. Help me to rely on Your strength, rather than my own, as I face challenges at work.

22. Father, protect me from spiritual attacks and help me to put on the full armor of God daily.

23. Lord, give me the patience and grace to deal with

difficult coworkers or superiors.

24. Enable me to be a peacemaker, fostering a harmonious and positive atmosphere at work.

25. Lord, grant me the discernment to recognize opportunities to share my faith with others.

26. Help me to be a good steward of my time and talents, using them for Your glory.

27. Father, let me be an example of integrity and honesty in all my dealings at work.

28. Strengthen my resilience in the face of setbacks, knowing You are with me.

29. Lord, help me to find rest in You, even during demanding and stressful times.

30. Grant me a spirit of contentment, being grateful for the work and opportunities You provide.

31. Lord, give me the courage to seek Your guidance and follow Your lead in all I do.

32. Father, let my words be filled with grace, encouragement, and love, reflecting Your heart.

33. Help me to be a servant leader, putting others' needs before my own.

34. Lord, guide me in using my gifts and talents to glorify You in my workplace.

35. Enable me to maintain a work-life balance, giving time to nurture my relationship with You.

36. Father, grant me divine appointments to share Your gospel with those around me.

37. Help me to be humble, acknowledging that my strength comes from You alone.

38. Lord, let Your peace guard my heart and mind, even in

stressful situations.

39. Strengthen my resolve to seek Your will and direction in every decision I make.

40. Enable me to cultivate a spirit of thankfulness, recognizing Your hand in all things.

41. Father, help me to be patient and kind, showing Your love to all I interact with.

42. Lord, grant me the ability to handle criticism and feedback with grace and humility.

43. Strengthen my faith to trust in Your provision and guidance, even in uncertain times.

44. Father, protect me from the lure of worldly success and keep my focus on eternal values.

45. Help me to be a source of encouragement to those who are struggling or discouraged.

46. Lord, grant me the boldness to speak up for what is right and just in my workplace.

47. Strengthen my commitment to honor You in all I do, even when no one is watching.

48. Lord, let my life be a reflection of Your goodness and grace to those around me.

49. Enable me to be a positive influence, inspiring others to seek You and Your truth.

50. Father, I commit my work and workplace into Your hands, trusting that You will be my strength and guide each day.

May these prayer points strengthen your spiritual life at your workplace and draw you closer to God as you seek to live out your faith in all aspects of your life.

Prayer for anxiety at workplace

1. Heavenly Father, I come before You, casting all my anxieties on You, knowing that You care for me. (1 Peter 5:7)
2. Lord, I confess that I am weak, but I know that Your strength is made perfect in my weakness. (2 Corinthians 12:9)
3. Grant me peace that surpasses all understanding, guarding my heart and mind in Christ Jesus. (Philippians 4:7)
4. Help me to trust in You with all my heart and lean not on my own understanding. (Proverbs 3:5)
5. Lord, deliver me from fear, for You have not given me a spirit of fear, but of power, love, and a sound mind. (2 Timothy 1:7)
6. Fill me with Your presence, knowing that You are with me wherever I go. (Joshua 1:9)
7. Father, help me to be anxious for nothing, but in everything, through prayer and supplication, let my requests be made known to You. (Philippians 4:6)
8. Grant me the wisdom to focus on the present moment and not be anxious about the future. (Matthew 6:34)
9. Lord, let Your perfect love cast out all my fears. (1 John 4:18)
10. Help me to remember that You are my refuge and strength, a very present help in trouble. (Psalm 46:1)
11. Father, fill my mind with thoughts that are true, noble, just, pure, lovely, and praiseworthy. (Philippians 4:8)
12. Lord, grant me the grace to surrender my worries to You

and find rest in Your arms. (Matthew 11:28)

13. Help me to keep my mind fixed on You, knowing that You will keep me in perfect peace. (Isaiah 26:3)

14. Father, remind me that You are in control, and nothing is too difficult for You. (Jeremiah 32:27)

15. Lord, enable me to be still and know that You are God. (Psalm 46:10)

16. Grant me the strength to resist the spirit of anxiety and embrace Your peace. (Galatians 5:22-23)

17. Help me to be confident in Your promises, knowing that You are faithful and true. (Hebrews 10:23)

18. Lord, lead me beside still waters and restore my soul. (Psalm 23:2-3)

19. Fill me with Your joy, for the joy of the Lord is my strength. (Nehemiah 8:10)

20. Father, help me to seek Your kingdom first and trust that all my needs will be provided. (Matthew 6:33)

21. Lord, let Your presence be a shield around me, keeping anxiety at bay. (Psalm 91:4)

22. Grant me the ability to cast down every anxious thought and bring every thought captive to the obedience of Christ. (2 Corinthians 10:5)

23. Help me to find comfort in Your Word, knowing that Your promises are true and reliable. (Psalm 119:50)

24. Lord, let Your grace be sufficient for me, for Your power is made perfect in weakness. (2 Corinthians 12:9)

25. Father, guide me in the path of righteousness, for Your name's sake. (Psalm 23:3)

26. Help me to meditate on Your goodness and faithfulness, for You have been my help in the past.

(Psalm 63:6-7)

27. Lord, grant me the peace that comes from knowing You, that nothing in this world can take away. (John 14:27)

28. Fill me with Your Spirit, so that I may bear the fruit of peace, even in the midst of challenges. (Galatians 5:22)

29. Father, remind me that I am fearfully and wonderfully made, and You have a purpose for my life. (Psalm 139:14)

30. Help me to release control and surrender my worries to You, trusting in Your perfect plan. (Proverbs 16:9)

31. Lord, enable me to be anxious for nothing but, through prayer and thanksgiving, present my requests to You. (Philippians 4:6)

32. Grant me the strength to take one step at a time, knowing that You are guiding my path. (Psalm 37:23)

33. Help me to abide in Your Word, for Your Word is a lamp to my feet and a light to my path. (Psalm 119:105)

34. Father, let Your peace rule in my heart, as I am called to peace and unity in Christ. (Colossians 3:15)

35. Lord, surround me with Your angels, protecting me from fear and anxiety. (Psalm 34:7)

36. Grant me the grace to surrender my cares and worries to You, knowing that You care for me. (1 Peter 5:7)

37. Help me to focus on the eternal rather than the temporal, fixing my eyes on things above. (Colossians 3:2)

38. Lord, remind me that You are my hiding place, and I can find refuge in You. (Psalm 32:7)

39. Fill me with Your peace that surpasses all

understanding, guarding my heart and mind. (Philippians 4:7)

40. Father, let me not be anxious about anything, but in everything, by prayer and supplication with thanksgiving, let my requests be made known to You. (Philippians 4:6)

41. Help me to be strong and courageous, knowing that You are with me wherever I go. (Joshua 1:9)

42. Lord, let Your joy be my strength, even in the face of challenges. (Nehemiah 8:10)

43. Grant me the grace to cast all my anxieties on You, knowing that You care for me. (1 Peter 5:7)

44. Help me to rest in Your promises, for You are faithful and true. (Hebrews 10:23)

45. Lord, let Your peace rule in my heart, for I am called to peace in one body. (Colossians 3:15)

46. Father, fill me with Your Spirit, that I may bear the fruit of peace and joy. (Galatians 5:22-23)

47. Help me to trust in Your provision and not worry about tomorrow. (Matthew 6:25-34)

48. Lord, let Your love cast out all my fears, for perfect love casts out fear. (1 John 4:18)

49. Grant me the grace to be anxious for nothing but, through prayer and supplication, present my requests to You. (Philippians 4:6)

50. Help me to set my mind on things above, not on earthly things, for my life is hidden with Christ in You. (Colossians 3:2-3)

May these scriptural prayer points bring comfort, peace, and the assurance of God's presence in your life, helping you to overcome anxiety and find strength in Him at your workplace.

Don't miss out!

Visit the website below and you can sign up to receive emails whenever Johannes Tefo publishes a new book. There's no charge and no obligation.

https://books2read.com/r/B-A-UEZX-BZAYC

BOOKS2READ

Connecting independent readers to independent writers.

Did you love *The Workplace You Need: Spiritual Warfare Prayers That Silence Evil Powers At Your Workplace.*? Then you should read *Children's Bread: Practical Deliverance Manual From Demons*[1] by Thabang Tefo!

[2]

Practical Deliverance from Demons is a powerful guide for anyone seeking to overcome the influence of malevolent spirits and experience true spiritual freedom. Drawing on decades of experience in ministry, the author provides a comprehensive roadmap for identifying and confronting demonic oppression in all its forms.

---

1. https://books2read.com/u/bQNErd

2. https://books2read.com/u/bQNErd

From understanding the biblical basis for spiritual warfare to developing a strategy for personal deliverance, this book covers all aspects of the deliverance process with clarity and practicality. You'll learn how to discern the signs of demonic influence in your life, how to break free from generational curses, and how to wield the authority given to you by Christ to command demons to leave.

But Practical Deliverance from Demons is more than just a how-to guide. It's a book that offers hope and encouragement to those who have been suffering under the weight of spiritual oppression. With powerful testimonies and real-life examples, the author shows how deliverance can bring lasting healing and freedom to individuals, families, and even entire communities.

Whether you're a seasoned believer or a skeptic seeking answers, Practical Deliverance from Demons is a must-read. It will equip you with the knowledge, tools, and confidence to stand firm against the forces of darkness and step into the fullness of God's plan for your life. Get your copy today and start your journey towards spiritual victory!

Also by Johannes Tefo

Family spiritual Warfare Books
Youth's Guide To Spiritual Warfare
A Women's Guide To Spiritual Warfare

Standalone
Deliver Your Soul From Evil
Overcoming Spirit Of Stagnation
The 24: Prophetic Word For This Season 2024 And Beyond
Michael For Warfare
Territorial Spirits: Overcome Evil Strongholds in Your Life And Take Over Your Community With Strategic Warfare And Winning Prayers
Prayers Against Suicide Spirit
Spiritual Warfare When Enough is Enough
Identity In Christ
Prayers Against Satanic Networks
The Workplace You Need: Spiritual Warfare Prayers That Silence Evil Powers At Your Workplace.

About the Author

Before he started writing Christian books, Johannes got a graduate degree in Film and Television from university of Johannesburg. After that, just to shake things up, he went to equip himself with religious studies, particularly Christianity, just to have knack about the world beyond the curtains of time. And how this body of Christ has transformed millions of people around the world, not neglecting how sadly the movement has been persecuted from time to time. He now writes full time.